I0177513

MEMOIR

ON THE

WESTERN OR EDOOR TRIBES

INHABITING THE SOMALI COAST OF N. E. AFRICA;

WITH THE SOUTHERN BRANCHES OF THE FAMILY OF DARROOD,

RESIDENT ON THE BANKS OF THE WEBBI SHEB EYLI,

COMMONLY CALLED THE RIVER WEBBI.

BY LIEUTENANT C. J. CRUTTENDEN, INDIAN NAVY,

ASSISTANT POLITICAL AGENT AT ADEN.

PRINTED FOR THE USE OF GOVERNMENT.

BOMBAY:

TIMES' PRESS—J. CHESSON, PRINTER.

1848.

MEMOIR

ON THE

WESTERN OR EDOOR TRIBES

INHABITING THE SOMALI COAST OF N. E. AFRICA;

WITH THE SOUTHERN BRANCHES OF THE FAMILY OF DARROOD,

RESIDENT ON THE BANKS OF THE WEBBI SHEBEYLI,

COMMONLY CALLED THE RIVER WEBBI.

DURING the time that I was employed at the wreck of the East India Company's Steam Frigate *Memnon*, at Ras Asseyr, on the N. E. coast of Africa, I employed myself in obtaining what information I could relative to the Tribes on the coast, which I had the honor to forward to Government on my return. As, however, I have since that time had further opportunities of visiting the different branches of the Somali tribes, I now beg to offer a few remarks in addition, relative chiefly to those tribes inhabiting the African coast westward from Burnt Island, and distinguished amongst the windward tribes as the " Edoor."

From Ras Hafoon, on the eastern coast, to Zeyla, the country is known by the name of the Bur-e-Somal, and it is divided into two great nations, who, both tracing their origin from the Arab province of Hadramant, are yet at bitter and endless feud with each other. The principal of these two great families is that to the eastward, or windward of

Burnt Island. It is divided into four large and three smaller tribes, as follows :—the Mijirtheyn, the Ahl Oor Sungeli or Wur Sungeli, the Dultahutah, and the Ahl Agahdur, forming the chief branches. Murrey-han, Girrhi, and Burtirrhi, the smaller ones. They claim as their common father Darrood, the son of Ismail, the son of Okeil, the son of Arab, who came from Hadramant, and, marrying a daughter of the Ha-weea tribe, residing on the N. E. coast of Africa, became the first Mahomedan founder of the Somali nation to the eastward—a nation extending to bunder Jedid or Burnt island to the eastward, and reaching as far as the northern Webbi river, or the Shebeyli to the southward.

The second of these two nations extends from Burnt island, or bunder Jedid, to Zeyla, and is divided into three great tribes, namely, the Haber Gerhajis, the Haber Awul, and the Habertel Jahleh, (Haber meaning the sons of,) who were the children of Isaakh by three wives—the said Isaakh having crossed over from Hadramant some time after his countryman had founded the nation to the eastward, and settled at the town of Meyet, near Burnt island, where his tomb exists to this day. Isaakh, finding his influence on the increase, owing to his intermarriage with a Galla tribe, made a sudden descent upon the neighbourhood of Berbera, then in the hands of a celebrated Galla chieftain, Sultan Harrireh (whose residence in a cave is still shewn, not far from Berbera,) and succeeded in obtaining possession of the country as far as Zeyla. The eldest branch, the Haber Gerhajis, was put in possession of the frontier mountains of Koobis and Woghur to the southward, and the other two brothers were placed on either side of them, the Haber Awul establishing themselves on the lowlands from Berbera to Zeyla, and Habertel Jahleh locating themselves at Kurrum, Enterad, Unkor, and Heis, four small ports to the eastward of Berbera. The Patriarch, Isaakh, was gathered to his fathers at a very advanced age, and was buried at the town of Meyet, leaving behind him a name which is honored and respected to this day.

The tract of country thus subdued yet remains in the hands of the posterity of Isaakh. The Galla tribes of the Esa Somal, and Gidr Beersi, to the westward, professed the faith of Islam, and were permitted to retain their possessions. Of these tribes, the Gidr Beersi limit the Hebrawul to the westward, and are themselves bounded by the Esa Somal, a very numerous horde, nominal Mahomedans, who extend as far as Hurrur to S. S. W., and to the borders of the Weima and Dunkali country to the westward. The remaining Galla tribes either became mixed up with their semi Arab conquerors, or were driven across the Webbi river. I ought to say one of the Webbi rivers, for there appear to be three or four, though the principal branch, and that to which I allude, is, doubtless, the Shebeyli, a river* taking its rise in the province of Gurague, and which, making a considerable curve to the N. and E., finally loses itself in the sand below Mukdesha, and not far from the sea.

In the meanwhile, the nations to the eastward had not been idle. The Mijirtheyn and Ahl Oor Sungeli secured the whole seaboard from Hafoon to bunder Jedid; the Dultahutah established themselves on the prairie land south of the lofty range of the Oor Sungeli mountains; the tribe of Murreyhan took possession of the country of Nogal, abounding in myrrh of the finest quality; whilst the Ahl Agahdur, Girrhi, and Burtirrhi, occupied the country to the westward, until they reached to the south of Berbera. The southern boundary of the four last named tribes of Darrood was the river Webbi, or Shebeyli, which thus defines the Somali country from near Mukdesha, on the eastern coast, to twelve days' journey S. S. W. from Zeyla.

The subdivisions of the three principal descendants of Isaakh are well known, as also are those of Darrood, but I have been able to glean only scanty information regarding the smaller and more distant tribes of Murreyhan, Girrhi, Burtirrhi, and Burzook. The Gidr Beersi and the Esa Somal have several peculiarities which mark their Galla origin. The Esa have three chiefs, each styled, in the language of the country, Oghass. Of these, Oghass Farah and Oghass Robeleh are the most powerful, their residence being in the neighbourhood of Hurrur, from the Emir of which place each annually receives a red flannel nightcap and a few pieces of cloth. " As treacherous as the Esa" is a proverb at Zeyla, whose inhabitants declare that their savage neighbours will give you a bowl of milk to drink with one hand, and stab you with the other. From my personal experience of them, I have but too much reason to consider them a cruel and treacherous race, amongst whom murder (the more atrocious the better) is at a premium, and who can in no way be trusted save at the expence of a heavy bribe.

* Called by Lieutenant Christopher the Hamess river. I am assured by many of the Somalis who have traded beyond Hurrur, that the three rivers, the Joeb or Webbi Ganana, the Shebeyli, and the Hawash, all take their rise in the mountains of Bugama.

The Gidr Beersi are a shade more civilized than the Esa, owing probably to their commingling more with the Somali tribes. Both the Esa and Gidr Beersi, however, scarcely deserve the name of Mahomedans, for hardly one in a hundred can pray, and reading and writing, save in the case of a few very learned men, are unknown. I have been assured by many of the Gidr Beersi that in the mountains forming the southern barrier of their country are many wonderful ruins of stone and chunam, the work of former ages, and abounding in inscriptions which no one can read. However tempting this description may appear, it must be received "cum grano," for, after a careful search along the coast from Cape Asseyr to Zeyla, I have not succeeded in finding any remains of antiquity, save the aqueduct at Berbera, elsewhere mentioned in this memoir, nor is it likely that an illiterate savage would be able to distinguish an inscription from an ornamental border on a stone. It is, however, to be hoped that an opportunity will be afforded of examining this very interesting country. Interesting it must be for many reasons : the possibility of inscriptions ; the extensive coffee districts ; the probability of the more northerly rivers that reach near the sea either flowing close round, or taking their rise in, the mountains ; and, further, the certainty that no European foot has hitherto traversed this part of the country.

The Esa tribe are generally at feud with their Hebrawul neighbours to the eastward. The number of horses that they possess renders their habits more predatory, if possible, than otherwise they would be ; and their forays are distinguished for the rapidity with which they are conducted, the secresy with which they are carried out, and the cold-blooded and ferocious conduct of the warriors engaged in the expedition. In February last year, a feud between two tribes near Berbera induced one, the Aial Yunus, to settle inland from a small roadstead called Bou'l Harr. Here a few traders joined them ; and, having left their women with the old men and children at the encampment inland, the men descended to the beach, to carry on their trade. Whilst thus employed, and unsuspicious of any danger, a foraying party or "Ghuzoo" of about 2,500 Esa Somalis attacked the camp inland, and put every one to the sword : men, women, and children, were indiscriminately massacred ; and, laden with an immense amount of booty, the plunderers reached their villages in safety. The Aial Yunus, paralysed by this catastrophe, were fain to send for assistance to their brethren at Berbera, and, marching shortly after inland, met with a fresh body of the Esa preparing to make a second descent, and slew above 650 men.

The city of Hurrur, in the province of that name, though hardly in the Somali country, is closely connected with it by its commerce, especially by its slave trade. Mr. McQueen, in his valuable Geographical survey of Africa, places it, in my opinion, too far to the southward and westward. It is eight days' journey for a kafila of camels from Zeyla to Hurrur, and nine days from Berbera, and this would place it in about Latitude 9°22′ N. and Longitude 42°35′ E.

A tradition exists amongst the people of Hurrur, that the prosperity of their city depends upon the exclusion of all foreigners not of the Moslem faith, and Christians are especially interdicted. From what I have been able to gather, the traveller would hardly be repaid for the risk and fatigue that he would have to undergo ; and if he travelled as an European, he would be exposed to much insult and ill feeling from the bigoted ruler and inhabitants of the place, who, sunk in the lowest ignorance, still plume themselves upon their superior sanctity as followers of the true faith.

The Government, founded, in all probability, during the reign of Suleiman the Magnificent, when the Turks held possession of Aden, is hereditary, and held by an Emir, all of whose male relatives, as was formerly the case in Shoa, are closely imprisoned, as a guard against domestic treachery. The Emir's house is perpetually surrounded with guards, and no one dares to pass the gate of the court-yard mounted, or at a walk—he must cover his face and run. The Emir's guard is composed of perhaps sixty matchlock-men, and he has also a body of native spearmen in his pay. A few rusty old iron guns, lying *outside* the walls, with their muzzles pointed towards the Galla country, are quite sufficient to keep those unruly savages from entering the city, but the flocks and herds are frequently carried off close to the walls.

The city is described as larger than Mokha, and situated in a fertile country, but fast decaying. Though many large and well-built houses of mud and stone are still to be found, the majority of the people live in huts made of mats and reeds, with a thorn fence round them. There are five gates to the town, viz., Bab Gooboi, Bab Joomboi, Bab Dimboi, Bab Budrobin, Bab Sukbakburri, the whole of which are locked nightly with the most jealous care, and the keys carried to the Emir's house,—a precaution which, seeing that about twenty yards of the wall is knocked down, appears rather excessive. The " Ashraffi," stamped at the Hurrur mint, is a coin peculiar to the place.* It is of silver, and is the twenty-second part of a dollar. The only specimen that I have been able to procure bore the date of 910 of the Hejira, with the name of the Emir on one side, and on its reverse "La Illahi il Ullah." The coffee districts are described as lying amongst a low range of mountains near Hurrur, and to the southward. The quantity exported is very large, and the quality fully equal to that commonly sold as "Mokha." Besides coffee, Hurrur exports white cotton cloths, used as dresses by the wealthiest classes. They are known by the name of "Tobe Hurruri," and consist of a double length of eleven cubits by two in breadth.† They have a deep border of various colors, of which some are very good, especially the scarlet. The cotton of which they are made is grown at Hurrur, and the price of really good dress is from five to eight dollars. On the windward coast one of these dresses is considered a handsome present for a chief, and I have been offered a horse in exchange for one of moderate quality. A few silk loongies are also manufactured at Hurrur, and I was assured that the silk is brought from the countries south of Shoa. Cardamoms, gum mastic, myrrh, a small quantity of manna, saffron, and safflower, with the articles abovementioned, comprise the extent of the Hurrur trade so far as regards produce, but the most valuable branch of commerce is the export of slaves from Gurague and Habesha.

The duties levied at Hurrur are ten per cent on imports and exports, and a further tax of six pounds of brass, or two and a half dollars, is laid on slaves of both sexes. The country in the vicinity is described as well watered and fertile, and between the city and port of Zeyla the traveller crosses six small mountain streams of inconsiderable magnitude flowing to the S. E., viz., Mugush, Shuktheyeh, Subbill, Shefee Amman, Billoo, and Hamer.

Zeyla, the sea port of Hurrur, but under the dominion of the Shereef of Mokha for the time being, is a miserable mud-walled town, containing some twelve to fifteen stone houses, 180 huts, and 750 souls. It is situated on a low sandy point nearly level with the sea, and its nearest well of drinkable water lies at a distance of seven miles. A vessel of 250 tons cannot approach within a mile of the town, and the anchorage is shallow, and difficult of entrance after sunset, on account of several

* The value of the Ashraffi changes with each successive ruler. In the reign of Emir Abd E. Shekoor, some 200 years ago, it was of gold.

† The Hurrur cloth is considered fully equal to that manufactured in Shoa.

reefs. Zeyla, no doubt, originally was intended to serve as a sea port for Hurrur, for, of itself, it appears to be worth little. There are no remains of antiquity to be found either in the town or neighbourhood, and I should not assign an earlier date to the settlement than A. D. 1500, or shortly after the occupation of Yemen by the Turks.

When the Turks were compelled to retire from Yemen, the town of Zeyla was subject to the Chief of Sana, who gave it in perpetuity to the family of a Sanani merchant, Syed-el-Bhor, in the hands of whose descendants it yet remains; but the kingdom of the Imam, like most other native principalities, having fallen into decay, the town is now under the authority of the Shereef of Mokha, who has the power of displacing the Governor, should he think fit, but who yet receives no part of the reve- nue. This is farmed out, and the present Chief, Hadj Shermarkhi Ali Saleh, pays annually to Syed Mahommed-el-Bhor, at Mokha, the sum of 750 German crowns, and reserves all that he can collect above that sum for himself.

The Governor has to provide fifty matchlockmen from the Arab coast to defend the town and well. They are paid on an average two and three quarter dollars per month in kind, and must find their own gun- powder. Occasional bribes are necessary to keep up the good feeling of the Shereef of Mokha and the men about him, and altogether the office of Governor at Zeyla must be as expensive as it is troublesome.

Zeyla levies a tax of one dollar upon each slave exported from Ta- joura, or imported from Hurrur, and afterwards sold at Berbera. For- merly Zeyla obtained but three quarters of a dollar per head, the Sultan of Tajoura receiving the remainder, but this has of late fallen into disuse.

With reference to the slave trade, the position of Zeyla is important. It is the sea port of Hurrur, and it commands Tajoura and Berbera, the only available places of export; and when the time arrives for the final suppression of the slave trade on the north-eastern coast of Africa, the numerous advantages held out by Zeyla will be duly appreciated. As I have shown, Hurrur depends for its foreign supplies solely on Berbera and Zeyla, and were these two ports cut off from the merchants, so far as regards the sale of slaves, it must prove a death blow to the slave com- merce through that province from Abyssinia and Gurague. Berbera once forbidden, Tajoura is the only remaining outlet, and that outlet, thanks to the marauding habits of the Esa Somal and others, is much more frequently closed than open.

With the above brief sketch I close my remarks on the Gidr Beersi and Esa Somal tribes, the western boundary of the Somali nation, and now beg to offer what information I have been able to collect relative to the three great tribes of Haber Gerhajis, Haber Awul, and Habertel Jahleh.

The Haber-awul, as I have before stated, occupied the low lands between Berbera and Zeyla, a fertile tract of country, with several low ranges of hills, and averaging perhaps forty miles in depth to ninety in length. The number of sheep, goats, she camels, &c., found on these plains, is perfectly incredible, fully realizing the account given of the flocks and herds of the patriarchs of old, for many of the elders of these tribes own each more than 1500 she camels, and their flocks of sheep are literally uncounted. Asses are very numerous, and most admirably adapted to the country. The camels are small and weak, and are never used for riding, except in a case of sickness, or a wound. The Haber-awul have no Chief. The customs of their forefathers are the laws of the country, and appear to be based upon the simple principle that might gives right. Theft is punishable with the loss of the right hand, and fortunate it is for the Haber-awul that this is not insisted upon, for they are the most inveterate thieves that I ever found on the coast. They wear the " Reesh," or Ostrich Feather, after slaying a man, but speak with abhorrence of the Esa custom of mutilation after (and sometimes before) death.

Two branches of the Haber-awul tribe, the Aial Ahmed * and the Aial Yunus, having established themselves at Berbera, took upon themselves the office of protecting strangers who annually visit that port during the time of the great fair. The " Abban," as the protector is called, is bound to arrange all disputes, and even fight all battles, that may arise between his client and his countrymen. In all sales or purchases he acts as broker, and in like manner does not forget to demand his brokerage. His food and lodging are provided at the expense of the merchant who employs him, and the office is considered honorable, as well as lucrative. The thieving propensities of the Haber-awul, above alluded to, are not indulged in in these cases, but should the merchant have the presumption to trust to himself, and to dispense with an " Abban," the chances are that he would be despoiled of all his goods.

The Aial Yunus, who are more numerous than the Aial Ahmed, for

* The following shews the descent of the Aial Ahmed and Aial Yunus from Isaakh :—Isaakh, Habir Awul, Musa, Saad, Isaakh, Awuth, Abou Bekr, Jibnil, Ismail, Noh, Yunus Ahmed, Aial Yunus, Aial Ahmed.

some years admitted them to equal participation in these profits, but after the occupation of Aden by the British, the office became more valuable, in consequence of the Aden Banians employing an "Abban" throughout the whole year, who, when the fair was over, proceeded inland with an investment of goods, and purchased, in anticipation, much of the produce of the future year.

Jealousies soon arose, and the Aial Yunus shortly after drove the Aial Ahmed out of Berbera, and declared themselves the only "Abbahs" for strangers during the fair. The Aial Ahmed upon this took advantage of Berbera being deserted as usual, and, with the assistance of Hadj Shermarkhi Ali Saleh, governor of Zeyla, erected four martello towers on the spot generally occupied by the town, and hired thirty matchlockmen to garrison them. A battle of course ensued, and, assisted by the foreign allies, the Aial Ahmed drove the Aial Yunus away from the place, with the loss of thirty-three killed and double that number wounded.

From this period the two tribes have been at deadly feud. The Aial Yunus established themselves at the roadstead of Bou'l Harr, about twenty-five miles to the westward of Berbera, and, from their influence and connections with the Indian merchants, succeeded in drawing a considerable portion of the trade to the new settlement.

Everything, however, turned against them. A gale of wind during one season destroyed seven native vessels fully laden, and the Esa Somal in February 1847 committed frightful slaughter amongst their women and children, compelling them to sue to the Aial Ahmed for assistance. The present season will, it is to be hoped, put an end to the feud. The Aial Ahmed will destroy their ports, and the trade will then be carried on as before; but amongst these savage tribes, promises are of no avail, and the slightest provocation, on either side, will be the signal for the renewal of hostilities.

The fair at Berbera is now so well known that it may appear superfluous to give any further description of it, but as it is the principal port in the Haber-awul country, a few remarks regarding it may not be considered out of place.

That Berbera has existed as a port of great trade for several centuries, I conceive to be almost sufficiently proved by the fact of its being an annual rendezvous for so many nations to the present day, and from the time for this great meeting having been chosen so as to suit the set of the Red Sea and Indian monsoons. But, with the exception of an aqueduct of stone and chunam, some nine miles in length, of which a short account will be found in another portion of this memoir, Berbera exhibits no proofs of antiquity; and the extraordinary remains of buildings, castles, reservoirs, &c., still found at the ancient emporia of Aden, Hisu Gherab, and Nukab-el-Hajar, have no place on the sandy shores of N. E. Africa.

The annual fair is one of the most interesting sights on the coast, if only from the fact of many different and distant tribes being drawn together for a short time, to be again scattered in all directions. Before the towers at Berbera were built, the place from April to the early part of October was utterly deserted, not even a fisherman being found there; but no sooner did the season change, than the inland tribes commenced moving down towards the coast, and preparing their huts for their expected visitors. Small craft from the ports of Yemen, anxious to have an opportunity of purchasing before vessels from the Gulf could arrive, hastened across, followed about a fortnight to three weeks later by their larger brethren from Muscat, Soor, and Ras-el-Khyma, and the valuable freighted bugalas from Bahrein, Bussorah, and Graen. Lastly, the fat and wealthy Banian traders from Porebunder, Mandavie, and Bombay, rolled across in their clumsy kotias, and with a formidable row of empty ghee jars slung over the quarters of their vessels, elbowed themselves into a prominent position in the front tier of craft in the harbour, and, by their superior capital, cunning, and influence, soon distanced all competitors.

During the height of the fair, Berbera is a perfect Babel in confusion, as in languages: no chief is acknowledged, and the customs of bygone years are the laws of the place. Disputes between the inland tribes daily arise, and are settled by the spear and dagger, the combatants retiring to the beach at a short distance from the town, in order that they may not disturb the trade. Long strings of camels are arriving and departing day and night, escorted generally by women alone until at a distance from the town; and an occasional group of dusky and travel-worn children marks the arrival of the slave kafila from Hurrur and Efât.

At Berbera, the Gurague and Hurrur slave-merchant meets his correspondent from Bussorah, Bagdad, or Bunder Abbas; and the savage Gidr Beersi, with his head tastefully ornamented with a scarlet sheepskin in lieu of a wig, is seen peacefully bartering his ostrich-feathers and gums with the smooth-spoken Banian from Porebunder, who, prudently living on board his ark, and locking up his puggree, which would infallibly be knocked off the instant he was seen wearing it, exhibits but a small portion of his wares at a time under a miserable mat shed on the beach.

By the end of March the fair is nearly at a close, and craft of all kinds, deeply laden, and sailing generally in parties of three or four, commence their homeward journey. The Soori boats are generally the last to leave, and by the first week in April Berbera is again deserted, nothing being left to mark the site of a town lately containing 20,000 inhabitants, beyond bones of slaughtered camels and sheep, and the framework of a few huts, which is carefully piled on the beach in readiness for the ensuing year. Beasts of prey now take the opportunity to approach the sea : lions are commonly seen at the town well during the hot weather ; and in April last year, but a week after the fair had ended, I observed three ostriches quietly walking on the beach. The great drawback to Berbera as a port is the scarcity of good water, that in the two wells belonging to the town being almost too brackish for use, and the wealtheir portion of the merchants are therefore compelled to send to Seyareh, a small harbour eighteen miles distant to the eastward, for a supply. I had frequently been told by the Somalis at Berbera that the remains of an ancient aqueduct were still to be seen, and, taking advantage of an unavoidable detention at that port, I visited the ruins, and satisfied myself that in former times water had been conveyed to the port by an aqueduct of nearly nine miles in length.

At the distance of half a mile from the beach I found the remains of a small building, apparently a mosque, and close to it a shallow reservoir, built of stone and chunam, having a channel leading into it of about twenty inches in diameter and twelve in depth. I opened this channel in two or three places, and found it of an uniform size and structure. At about seven yards from the reservoir it was lost for some distance, but by walking in the direction of the nearest range of hills, known as Dthubar, slabs of limestone, and fragments of chunam, served to shew the general course of the aqueduct ; and at about a mile from the hill of Dthubar, it was again found entire for several yards. The cement used was as hard as the stone itself, and, as usual in all ancient remains in this part of the world, mixed with large pebbles. Many graves are observed in the neighbourhood, and the stones of the aqueduct had been used to form the tombs.

Half a mile from these remains I arrived at a swamp, having at the upper end a spring of water, which, when I last visited the place, shewed a temperature of 107° Fahrenheit, whilst the thermometer in the open air stood at 76°. The water was slightly bitter, and in quality highly astringent.

The remains of a small fort or tower, of chunam and stone, were found on the hill side immediately over the spring. In style it was different to any houses now found on the Somali coast. It would not contain more than ten or twelve men, and I imagine must have been intended as a kind of guard-house over the spring. On a hill to the N. E. of this, several small houses were found, each having a semicircular niche on the north side, similar to the prayer niche of the Mussulmans, but these again were built of loose stones, and I have seen others like them on the coast to the eastward of Berbera. Crossing the shoulder of the hill, another spring was found, apparently of rather better quality than the former, and which was the nightly resort of the wild ass, the ostrich, and the onyx, numbers of which were seen on the plains.

In the neighbourhood of the fort abovementioned abundance of broken glass and pottery was found, and from this I should infer that it was a place of considerable antiquity; but, though diligent search was made, no traces of inscriptions could be discovered.

The hill immediately over the spring is of moderate height, and of limestone formation, having many shells imbedded. Gypsum is found in large quantities, and from its unusual hardness I imagine that it has been used as cement for the aqueduct. There is no doubt but that the water from this spring was carried down by this channel to the town, inasmuch as no other water could be found at the termination of the ruins. The nearest part of the aqueduct yet remaining is fully one-third of a mile from the swamp, and at a higher level. I am not certain if the spring is likewise below the level of the ruins, but no traces of chunam or of any channel could be found near it. The nation, however, who could construct an aqueduct of so great a magnitude, would not find much difficulty in raising water to a higher level. The fact of the aqueduct being thus established, it remains now to discover what nation could have constructed, and at what time the commerce of Berbera was sufficiently important to warrant, so costly an undertaking.

In the size of its channel, and in its mode of construction, the Berbera aqueduct is similar to that near Aden, excepting that in the former case stone is used, and in the latter brick.

The Aden aqueduct was built during the reign of El Malck Mausur Taj-é-Deen Abdul Wahab-ibu-Taher, Imam of Sana and Yemen, in the year of Christ 1470. This Prince appears to have spent large sums in beautifying the different towns of Yemen, having constructed many reservoirs, mosques, and aqueducts, in other parts also; but the Arab manuscripts give no account of the Imams of Yemen ever having assumed authority over, or extended their conquests to, the Somali coast: and though Aden was, at that time, one of the chief halting-places in the then great commercial highway of the world, had the Arabs taken possession of Berbera, there would have been some traces of them to this day. With the exception of a brief period, A.D. 1173, when Aden was taken by the brother of Saleh-é-Deen of Egypt, we have no mention of its having been governed by other than Arab Rulers until it submitted to Sulliman Pasha in A. D. 1538; and, as Arabs are not in the habit of expending money for the benefit of other countries, and we have no mention of their ever having resided at Berbera, the credit of the Berbera aqueduct would appear to be due to the Turks during the hundred years that they held Yemen.

But we are informed that A. D. 522 the Persian troops in the reign of Amishirwan drove the Abyssinian invaders of Yemen out of the country, and re-established a Hirnyari Prince on the throne of his father as a vassal of the Persian monarch; and Gibbon supposes that two years were consumed in this invasion of Yemen. Amishirwan was distinguished for his generous and wise government,—for the splendour of his public buildings, and especially for his aqueducts. The Persian troops on their arrival at Aden found a nation equalling themselves in civilization, and, as the ruins of Mareb Nukab-el-Hajar, and the unexplored cities of Hadramant, testify, skilled in architecture. To this date should I attribute the construction of the Berbera aqueduct. The trade carried on by the Red Sea was in those days great; the ancient emporia of Hisu Gherab and Aden prosperous and wealthy; and Berbera then, doubtless, carried on the same trade in ivory, gums, and ostrich feathers, that it does now. Lastly, I may observe that the chunam or lime used in the reservoir and aqueduct at Berbera is stated to be similar to the " Kutch or Gutch" of Persia.

During a short journey in 1847 I found the country inland from the hill of Dthubar consisting of low and undulating limestone ranges, thickly covered with tamarisk and acacia trees, and on the sides of the hills with the gum arabic. At the distance of two hours from Dthubar, I reached the pass of " Gudh Harrireh," in which is to be seen a large cave, said to have been in former times the residence of the Galla Chief Harrireh, who was expelled from the country by the descendants of Isaakh. The rock at this part is exceedingly pure and white limestone, and would be invaluable in Aden were it not for the expense of carriage. In the valley close to the pass, red granite, porphyry, white marble, and large fragments of gypsum, are common. It is worthy of remark that the gum arabic tree at Berbera differs in every way from that exported from the windward coast, the leaf and the tree both being smaller and of a different shape. The plain beyond this valley, extending one hour's journey S.S.W., is infested with lions, hyenas, and leopards, and it is considered unsafe for a single individual to cross it at night. The Somalis who accompanied me when I visited this part of the country formed a stout thorn fence round the baggage to keep off the lions, who came close round us during the night, but who left us in peace as soon as they heard the report of my carbine, which my followers, taking advantage of my having dropped asleep, fired off, much to my annoyance.

At the southern extremity of this plain I reached the valley of Dunanjir, a steep ravine, having in its bed a few pools of very bad and stinking water, almost unfit for man to drink, but which, nevertheless, proved most acceptable to us after a hot and fatiguing march. Passing over several low ranges of limestone, through which in many places red granite had been thrust, I reached another water-course, having very steep banks of thirty to forty feet high, thickly wooded, and having a most picturesque appearance. The bed of the water-course was of soft white sand, in any part of which water was procurable by scooping a hole a foot in depth. On the range of mountains between Dunanjir and this valley, I observed many large blocks of very pure white marble, with an abundance of obsidian gypsum, and large masses of basalt. The geological formation of the country appeared to be entirely without order, and led to the idea that, by some extraordinary convulsion of nature, rocks of all kinds had been thrown together in one large confused heap. A huge natural cairn might be observed of thirty to forty feet high, composed of six or seven different species of stone, a block of marble lying over or under an equally large boulder of red granite, and flanked, perhaps, by a fragment of conglomerate or black basalt.

This valley is much infested with lions, leopards, &c., and the traces of elephants were numerous. The diameter of the lion's foot was five and a half inches, and of the elephant, after several measurements, twenty-two inches, which would give a height of upwards of ten feet at the shoulder. This water-course passes round the western flank of the Dunanjir range, and can be traced down to the sea close to the town of Berbera. After heavy rains, it discharges a large body of water into the bay.

" From this valley, my course lay over a rough and stony tract of country, in many places well wooded and watered, but, so far as regards its formation, exhibiting, if possible, a still stranger appearance than the valley above mentioned. Thousands of ant hills, rising like slender sandstone pillars, and in many cases fourteen feet high, were scattered in every direction, giving the country the appearance of an immense Turkish cemetery: many were hollowed out entirely, others were pierced with smaller channels longitudinally, and a current of hot air could be detected rushing through.

On first seeing these columns, I fancied that I had reached some ancient ruins, so numerous were they. In one instance, I observed a huge block of marble, weighing many tons, having three or four of these sand pillars round it, and bearing the exact appearance of a tomb. On the brink of a cliff close by, an enormous rock, of perhaps eighteen to twenty feet in diameter, and diamond-shaped, stood exactly balanced on its point, and to all appearance required but a push to send it down into the ravine below. The number of graves found in every direction, excited my surprise. They were well built, and bore marks of great antiquity, but no inscriptions were found on them. Night closed in before we reached the plain of Shimberali, and we were glad to find an empty sheep-fold to shelter us for the night, after a march of seventeen hours on foot, of which three only could be spared for a halt during the greatest heat of the day.

Shimberali is part of an extensive plain, reaching from a solitary hill, called Deimoli, to the southern mountain range of Koobis, and Woghur, the frontier of the Haber Gerhajis tribe. It is inhabited by the Esa Moosa branch of the Haber Awul, who are looked upon by the elder branches of the tribe as a treacherous race, with whom it is advisable to keep on good terms, and who in their turn are at deadly feud with a branch of the Haber Gerhajis, residing on the mountains above them, and known as the Sulhehgiddib.

The plain is tolerably well wooded in some parts. Several varieties of gum trees are found : the mimosa, tamarisk, wild fig, and several species of the cactus and aloe, are abundant ; and in the deep fissures and rents made in the plain by the fury of the mountain torrents, a few dome and date trees are found. Elephants, lions, leopards, hyenas, wolves, and jackals, are to be seen on the plain, and occasionally a troop of ostriches. Salt's white antelope, the " sagarro" of the Somali, the koodoo, the kevel or scimitar-horned antelope, and the onyx, were the varieties of the deer species observed ; and the small antelope, or gazelle, was very common. Jerboas and squirrels were numerous, and a species of toucan. The white vulture, of enormous size, and the common osprey, were the principal birds observed. In the hot season much inconvenience is occasioned by a species of hornet, the " dibber" of the Somali, and the zinib (?) of Bruce, who justly styles them a curse. The same evil extends along the whole coast during the S. W. monsoon, where the slaughtering a sheep brings the hornets round in myriads, and very shortly compels the unlucky traveller to shift his position as fast as possible from the neighbourhood of his Somali butcher.

The hill of Deimoli is a lofty conical mountain, in many parts inaccessible. It is a great resort for beasts of prey, especially for lions, and is therefore avoided by the shepherds. It is apparently of limestone, and thickly wooded. At its base stands a smaller hill, bare and barren, and bearing a most extraordinary appearance, from its being scolloped in regular furrows by the action of the rain from top to bottom. On every side of Deimoli huge masses of rock lie piled on each other, and in many of these nature appears to have indulged in the wildest vagaries. Several of these masses formed perfect funnels, and others exhibited a smooth round basin on their upper surface, capable of containing many hundred gallons of water.

From the shoulder of Deimoli I was able to sketch the course of the valley and water-course abovementioned. For some distance on the plain (two to three hundred yards) it exhibits a running stream, when it is lost in the sand for perhaps the same distance, and then re-appears as before. In almost every part of its bed, water is procurable by digging a foot deep. Large bullrushes and tall wiry grass grow in rank luxuriance on its banks, affording a good retreat for the wild pig, one long-legged specimen of which was seen and missed by me on my return. Snakes are reported to be numerous, but I saw none.

After a long and fruitless search after the elephants, a herd of which seven in number, had passed a few hours before, and, after spending the night in the bed of a dry mountain torrent, I crossed over in a N. E. direction to examine another running stream, where I found excellent water falling down shelving linestone rock, forming pretty cascades, and collected into a tolerably large stone basin, the overflowings of which were lost in the sand. A large tree, from which depended a great many nooses of cord, attracted my attention, and I was told that once a year all the Bedouin families meet here, and each kills a sheep, which is hung up to one of these nooses, and then eaten, in common with the others. It is an observance intended to renew their friendship and acquaintance with each other, and as an opportunity of marrying their young people. On my return to Dthubar, I crossed over the Dunanjir range more to the eastward, and found them of the same formation as the hills I had observed on my way to Shimberali. The distance travelled over in this walk I compute at about seventy miles.

At a future period, accompanied by Commander C. D. Campbell, of the Indian Navy, I left Dthubar, and, after walking in a north-westerly direction, across a broad plain covered with ostriches, onyxes, koodoos, and quaggas, but all of whom, save the latter, were too shy to admit of our approaching within shot, we reached the bed of a broad water-course, having in its centre a stream of perhaps eight to ten feet in breadth, which at the distance of a mile below is absorbed in the sand. The native tradition says that the stream runs only by night, and from this it takes its name, " Bheeyeh Ghora"—" night-running water." The actual increase in the distance, occasioned doubtless by the evaporation being so great during the day, we found by measurement to be 135 yards, but the stream had then dwindled down to a mere thread. The temperature of the stream at seven A. M. was 69°, in the open air 71°. Following up the bed of this stream towards the hills, we observed in many spots the ground white with the efflorescence of nitre : the bitter taste of the water was thus accounted for. As we approached the narrow defile in the hills, through which the stream passed, pure salt was found adhering to the smooth sandstone rocks, generally encrusted on a dark-coloured vein, from which water exuded, and shortly after we reached a powerful hot spring, shewing a temperature of 125°, the thermometer in the open air standing at 76°.

Above this hot spring the valley became narrower, and, from the sandstone and limestone sides of the ravine, water was observed at almost every yard, dropping and forming large and beautiful stalactites. But what was most singular, though the rock throughout was the same, a hot spring of water would be found within a yard or two of another of cold water, and though the hot springs were disagreeable to the taste, the water obtained from those that were cold was sweet and good.

Fully a hundred of these springs exist in this valley, and the temperature of the main stream varied from 91° to 105°, the highest temperature found in any of the hot springs being 125°, and the water appearing to be strongly impregnated with iron.

A peculiar kind of creeper grows in great luxuriance in the neighbourhood of the springs, which in every case ooze through the rocks. The dragon's-blood tree was observed on the hills above, and an ibis and a coney were seen, whilst a flock of large apes noisily resented our intrusion upon their retirement. The head of the stream, I was assured, was to be found in the mountain range of Woghur, which I have since personally ascertained to be the fact. Near where the stream is lost in the sand we found an extensive burial-ground; and the remains of several old buildings of small dimensions, of no great antiquity. The distance of Bheeyeh Ghora from the sea is not great,—perhaps six miles; and I have been assured by several respectable natives, that on the sea shore north of Bheeyeh Ghora, and at the spot where its waters are discharged into the ocean after heavy rains, the remains of an ancient reservoir and aqueduct are to be found, similar to that previously described as extending from Dthubar to Berbera.

It is worthy of remark that the majority of the streams running from the mountain ranges of Woghur and Koobis are bitter, and in quality highly astringent. There are, however, others that afford most delicious and pure water, to be properly appreciated only after a seven years residence at Aden. The country to the south is described as an inclined plain, without hill or rock, for seven days' journey, and, on arrival at the province of Agahdur, we were told that stones sufficient to make a fireplace were not to be found, whilst the country was one immense prairie of some twenty days' extent.

The Haber Gerhajis, the eldest branch of the three tribes of Edoor, reside chiefly in the mountains to the south of Berbera, whence they extend to the country of Agahdur. They are a powerful and warlike tribe, numbering many horses, in addition to their flocks and herds, and have a nominal Sultan, who possesses, however, but little influence or power over his savage subjects. From this branch of the family of Isaakh sprung the venerable saint " Aber Khudli," whose tomb, S. W. from Berbera two days' journey, is yet the rendezvous when any grave question arises affecting the interests of the Edoor tribes in general. On a paper yet carefully preserved in the tomb, and bearing the sign manual of Belal, the slave of one of the early Khaleefehs, fresh oaths of lasting friendship, and alliances, are made,—to be broken again, as usual, without a shadow of provocation. In the season of 1846, this holy relic was brought to Berbera in charge of the Haber Gerhajis, and on it the rival tribes of Aial Ahmed and Aial Yunus swore to bury all animosity, and live as brethren in future—with how much sincerity, the events of the two succeeding seasons amply shew, some scores of lives having been lost on both sides.

In the country of the Haber Gerhajis, the principal articles of trade or produce are ghee principally, myrrh in small quantities, and of quality inferior to that produced in Agahdur and Murreyhan, luban of the first quality, ivory, ostrich-feathers, and gum arabic, with a small quantity of " shenna" or orchilla weed, and a still smaller supply of " warus"—a kind of saffron, used by the natives in Yemen to rub over their bodies.

The kafilas from the banks of the Webbi Shebeyli, from the small province of Gunana to the south of the above river, and from Agahdur, pass through the country of Haber Gerhajis on their way to Berbera, excepting the slave kafila from Abyssinia. These are the most valuable caravans of the season, bringing ivory from the Galla tribes of Sidama, south of the Webbi Gunana, ostrich-feathers, musk, myrrh, and frankincense. They frequently exceed 2000 camels in number, and are well guarded by the men of Agahdur, who may always be recognized amidst the crowd at Berbera by the red colour of their robes, produced, as they all declare, by the fine red dust peculiar to their country.

From Gunana to Berbera is twenty-four days for a kafila; from the Webbi Shebeyli nineteen days; and from Agahdur nine days. I consider the journey fully practicable for an European, if at all known to the Somali tribes on the coast; and in the more distant province of Agahdur his reception would be kind, and his person and property safe. In the small map of N. E. Africa appended to this memoir will be seen the position of the different tribes north of the Webbi Shebeyli, and my idea of the course of that river from Zeyla down to below Mukdesha. My information has been obtained from many natives of different tribes, and by comparing one with the other, no very serious error can arise in a journey of twenty days, when the country, after the first ranges are surmounted, presents a level for several days.

Amongst the Edoor tribes, as with the descendants of Darrood, there exists a class of men who never carry the spear and shield, but whose sole arms are the bow and poisoned arrow. With a couple of arrows in his mouth, and half a dozen more dangling from his long tangled hair, the " Rahini" is feared alike by man and beast, and in all forays is looked upon as an invaluable ally. Inferior in caste, and not ranking with the gentle blood of the Somali aristocracy, the "Rahini" approaches in every respect to the freedman of the Romans. They are expert and daring hunters, crippling the elephant by a blow on the back sinew with a heavy knife,* and attacking even the stately African lion with no better arms than the tiny though unerring "nishab," or arrow.

The tree from which the poison is made I found in the mountains of the Ahl Oor Sungeli, and at Aden I had a small quantity of poison prepared by a cunning Rahini, in my own house. Its effects on an animal are instantaneously fatal, and I have been repeatedly assured that on a human being the poison has equal power, causing the hair and nails to drop off, and the sufferer to die in less than half an hour. The only cure is immediate excision of the part wounded, and the number of ghastly scars visible on the bodies of the Somalis amply testifies to the dread in which the poisoned barb of the arrow is held amongst them.

This poison I imagine to be the same as that described by Major Sir W. Cornwallis Harris, in his work on South Africa, when speaking of the arms of the "Burhman," except that amongst the Rahinis the juice of the euphorbium is not made use of.

The last branch of the western tribes is the Haber-tel-Jahleh, who possess the sea ports from Seyareh to the ruined village of Rukudah, and as far as the town of Heis. Of these towns, Kurrum is the most important, from its possessing a tolerable harbour, and from its being the nearest point from Aden, the course to which place is N. N. W.,—consequently the wind is fair, and the boats laden with sheep for the Aden market pass but one night at sea, whilst those from Berbera are generally three. What greatly enhances the value of Kurrum, however, is its proximity to the country of the Dulbahanta, who approach within four days

* This was seen by Commander Campbell and myself when inland from Berbera ; and Bruce again has spoken only the truth.

of Kurrum, and who therefore naturally have their chief trade through that port. The Ahl Yusuf, a branch of the Haber-tel-Jahleh, at present hold possession of Kurrum, and between them and the tribes to windward there exists a most bitter and irreconcileable feud, the consequence of sundry murders perpetrated about five years since at Kurrum, and which hitherto have not been avenged.

The small ports of Enterad, Unkor, Heis, and Rukudah, are not worthy of mention, with the exception of the first-named place, which has a trade with Aden in sheep, and leaving the Haber-tel-Jahleh at Heis, therefore, it remains but to notice the ancient settlement of Meyet, the burial-place of the founder of the Edoor nation, and their present limit to the eastward. Meyet is situated on a small plain bounded on the South and S. W. by the western extreme of the lofty mountains of the Ahl Oor Sungeli, which here approach within two hours of the sea. From Meyet a large quantity of white ebony is exported, as also a long and thin rafter used both at Aden and on the Coast in the construction of native houses. The hills immediately over the town afford a large supply of very fine gums, and the place carries on a considerable trade with both Aden and Makulla.

The stranger is at once struck with the magnitude of the burial-ground at Meyet, which extends for fully a mile each way. Attachment to the memory of their forefather Isaakh yet induces many aged men of the western tribes to pass the close of their lives at Meyet, in order that their tombs may be found near that of their chief; and this will account for the unusual size of this cemetery. Many of the graves have head-stones of madrepore, on which is cut in relief the name of the tenant below; and of these many are to be found 250 years old.

In my notice of the western tribes, I have made use of the word Edoor to distinguish the descendants of Isaakh from those of his fellow-countryman Darrood, but it may be as well to observe that the western tribes are averse to the appellation, and invariably correct the person who styles them Edoor, by telling him that they (the Edoor) are the Galla tribes. The Mijirtheyn told me that the Galla family into which Sheikh Isaakh married was called " Durr," and from that is derived the name of " Edoor"; and the Haber Gerhajis, on the other hand, retaliate by quoting " Darrood" as an offshoot from the same pagan source.

I found it impossible to obtain any estimate of the number of their tribes, but the population in the interior is doubtless very great. The advantage that is almost universally taken of the liberal allowance of wives sanctioned by the Prophet, and the prolific character of the Somali females, is of itself a strong argument to that effect; but it would be idle to attempt to put down any fixed number as the population of this part or N. E. Africa, and I much doubt if all the tribes were computed separately, from report, whether we should even then obtain an approximate of the truth.

With this brief memoir of the Somali Tribes to the Westward of the town of Meyet, I now beg to offer what information I have been able to gather relative to the Southern Tribes bordering on the river Webbi.

To the South and S. S. West of Berbera, on the road to Hurrur, the kafilas pass through the country of the Burtirrhi and Girrhi, the two most western branches of the family of Darrood. Of these two tribes little is known. The Emirs of Hurrur have for many years intermarried with the Burtirrhi, and this gives them a certain degree of influence, but they no not visit the sea coast so commonly as the other tribes, and appear to be a pastoral race, occupied solely in tending their flocks and herds, and in planting the coffee tree on the low ranges south-east of Hurrur.

They are bordered on the S. E. and E. by the province of Agahdur, —a country of considerable extent, bounded on the south by the Webbi, and on the east by Murreyhan. From Berbera to Agahdur is nine days, of which I am assured that four are without water. The fertile valley of the Nogál passes Agahdur on its northern side; and throughout the province generally the ground is cultivated, and large quantities of white jowari is grown, forming the common food of the people.

Agahdur is stated to be a level country, possessing excellent pasturage for cattle, with abundance of water, which is procured by digging wells six to eight feet in depth. The soil is remarkable for its redness, but the purity of the air is highly extolled. From the number of their flocks and herds, the inhabitants, as might be expected, export large quantities of ghee from Berbera, and carry on a regular trade with the Galla tribes to the southward of the Webbi Shebeyli, through the intervention of the people resident at Gunana, who act as brokers on the occasion. The goods carried down for barter are white and blue cloth, cowries and beads, on which last an enormous profit is realised. The gums are purchased by the skin of sixty lbs., ostrich-feathers by the pound, and ivory by the frasila of twenty lbs.—if of large quality, and good of its kind.

The Galla tribes are described as a nation to be trusted if once an acquaintance is formed. They appear to understand cultivation of the soil, and produce immense quantities of jowari, which is retailed at a cheap rate on the east coast of Africa at the ports of Mukdesha, Juba, Putta, Lamoo, &c., and thence exported to Hadramant. Bruce mentions the river Webbi Gunana, or Jub, as the Yas, or Webbi ; and as an additional instance of his general veracity as a traveller, I may mention, that on my enquiring about this name from the Somali who recently had returned from the river, he told me that it was occasionally termed so from the stream being full of " Yahass" or alligators, rendering its navigation on a raft highly dangerous. From the word " Yahass," Bruce doubtless derives his name. It is now well known that " Webbi," in the Somali language, means a river, whilst Kebber or Kibbee signifies the bed of a river in which pools of water are found. After a long search after it, I found, by accident, that the river " Durdur," said to exist four days' inland from Burnt Island, meant, in the language of the country, a " running stream," but no river ; and doubtless, as our acquaintance with this part of the country increases, we shall find that the confusion now existing relative to the " Webbi" will be satisfactorily cleared up, and the number of rivers laid down in Mr. McQueen's map reduced to two only—the Jub, or the Webbi Gunana, and its northern brother the Webbi Shebeyli,—the three smaller streams running between them not being worthy of mention.

Agahdur is governed by a Chief who takes the title of Oghass, but who, like all other Somali Chiefs, can boast of little save the name. Horses are described as being abundant, and very cheap ; camels equally so. The country, by all accounts, is safe, and the climate healthy ; and a journey through Agahdur, down to Gunana, or down the Wadi Nogál, would amply repay the traveller. Amongst the families of Darrood, Agahdur ranks as second ; but in numerical strength, and extent of country, it would probably take the first place.

Of Murreyhan* but little is known. Bordering as it does on the Haweea tribe, who are a different caste of people to the Somalis, they are not looked upon with much consideration, but their country must abound in gums, myrrh, and ivory. The valley of the Nogál borders upon them, and they are separated from the sea by a belt of country occupied by the tribe of the Haweea,—the first connecting link between the Somali and the Seedie of the coast of Suwahhil.

* Murreyhan—a pompous man, a boaster.

Murreyhan cultivates no grain, and is separated from the Shebeyli River by the Haweea again. Kafilas from this province annually arrive at Berbera, bringing the best of myrrh, and the finest ostrich-feathers and ivory. Their breed of horses is highly esteemed, and I believe that a traveller might penetrate the country with ease, provided he took the precaution of being passed from tribe to tribe,—a measure indispensable amongst the Arabs, and highly desirable amongst the more savage inhabitants of north-east Africa.

Between Murreyhan and the country of the Ahl Oor Sungeli lie the great pasture ranges of the Dulbahanta,* a level country, abounding in grass, water, and timber, and without a stone. Unlike their other brethren, the Dulbahanta are a nation who fight chiefly on horseback, their arms being two spears and a shield. Their horses are powerful and courageous, —the breed descended, according to Somali tradition, from the stud of Suleiman the son of David, and consequently highly valued. The Dulbahanta, as far as I have seen of them, are a fine martial race of men, second to none of the branches of Darrood either in conduct or appearance, and they are described as being courteous and hospitable to the stranger who visits them. They have generally two Sultans, or Gerads, the elder of whom, Mahomed Ali Harrain, governs the eastern limits of the province; whilst his colleague, Ali Gerad, (recently deceased) guards the N. W. frontier from the thieving Haber-tel-Jahleh in the neighbourhood of Kurrum and from the Agahdur family of Noh Amor.

The Dulbahanta have no grain whatever, and subsist chiefly on milk alone, save when want of rain renders it necessary to thin the countless flocks and herds that roam over their boundless prairies. They have but few gums, but they bring down ivory, ostrich-feathers, and ghee, in abundance. Wild beasts are numerous—the lion especially so. The cameleopard (Somarilice, geerhi) is found on the grassy plains trending down to the southward from the stupendous mountain chain of the Jebel Ahl Oor Sungeli; and the koodoo, the onyx, and the black rhinoceros, are also common in the same neighbourhood.

North of the Dulbahanta, the country, for so great a distance level, begins to rise gradually. The grassy plains become more rocky; small limestone ranges are passed; until at last the level plateau of the Jebel Ahl Oor Sungeli is attained, when the traveller, from the dizzy brink of Eyransid (the cloud-bearer,) looks down a steep precipice of 1500 to

* Dulbahanta—outnumbering and excelling all.

2000 feet, and sees the villages of the Ahl Oor Sungeli dotted along the sandy sea coast 6500 feet below him.

This magnificent range, so aptly named, and rising in solemn grandeur about twenty-five miles from the sea, had long been looked at from a distance by me; and a visit to the Gerad, or chief of the Ahl Oor Sungeli, in February, 1848, afforded me the opportunity so long coveted of visiting them. Between Mahomed Ali Gerad and myself frequent friendly letters and messages had passed, by means of the boats that touched at his ports on their way to Aden, and during this, my first, interview with him, he appeared anxious to get "his name written in the good books of the English" as his Mijirtheyn brothers had done. An assurance that I might go anywhere I pleased over his country, was caught at on my part with a readiness that appeared rather to alarm him, but seeing that my tent and travelling kit was already on its way to the shore, he apparently thought it useless to argue the matter or magnify the perils of the road. By the following afternoon we had left the town of Ras Kori, and, taking a small guard of elders from his own tribe, we bid His Majesty an affectionate farewell, and turned our steps in the direction of the lofty barrier range of Eyransid.

An hour's sharp walking took us some distance up the bed of a watercourse having a general southerly direction, and the night was passed in a small clearing under the cliff. At sunrise the march was resumed, and, passing some three to four miles up the same water-course, in which we observed several large monkeys and some remarkably fine antelopes, we crossed a low shoulder covered with gum trees, amongst which we found the myrrh, and had an opportunity of collecting a small portion of its gum. It was the same tree as that sent down by me to Bombay some years ago, and the only one, as I was assured, affording the myrrh of commerce. Entering the bed of the mountain torrent a second time, we observed the broad-leafed luban tree (meyeti), the wadi and adadi species of the gum arabic, and large specimens of the harraz, or baabul tree. The sides of the water-course were regularly-disposed strata of fine and coarse gravel, interspersed with huge boulders of limestone. Fragments of porphyry were frequently picked up, and small quantities of pure white marble. Shortly before nine we reached a pool of water in the bed of the mountain torrent, which had a decidedly bitter taste, similar to that before described at Bheeyeh Ghora. The temperature was pleasant, not exceeding 81° under a tent at seven A. M. The general direction of the water-course during this march was north and south.

By three in the afternoon we were once more on our way. The ascent became very steep, and we now came upon large fragments of iron-stone, interspersed with lava and black basalt: small masses of red ochre were common, as also hardened clay; and the frankincense tree now began to be very abundant. A most fatiguing ascent of two hours exhausted man and beast, and, too tired to trouble ourselves about the tent, we lay down on the mountain side under the lee of an ancient burial-ground, and with the thermometer down to 65°, and the clouds rolling round us, were drenched to the skin with the dew.

The hour for morning prayer found us packed up and on our road. For three hours we crossed over undulating hills, every mile rapidly increasing the elevation. The dragon's-blood tree now appeared in abundance, and, from my former experience amongst the Mijirtheyn, I was not surprised to find that its value was unknown in the Oor Sungeli country. The "bochain" of Socotra, a peculiar tree found also in Aden, but I believe possessing no generic name, was seen on every side; and another extraordinary specimen, like a gigantic bulb of three to four feet in diameter, with a few small sprouts not worthy of the name of branches, springing from its top, attracted our attention, at an estimated height of 4000 feet. We halted during the heat of the day, with the thermometer 76° at noon. The country now began to assume the general character of a limestone range. The water-course that we had left the day previous was to be seen winding its way into the ravines of the high range, and here and there a cluster of white limestone slabs pointed out the site of an ancient graveyard.

At three P.M. the ascent was resumed. The country became more thickly wooded, and more beautiful, as we advanced. The track of the rhinoceros warned us to have our rifles in readiness, and before sunset we pitched on a small level spot of ground, about 1000 feet below the peak of Eyransid. A stream of delicious water was found within half a mile of the tent, the only drawback upon which was that it abounded in small leeches, which rendered it necessary to be cautious in drinking without due examination. The tree, from the root of which is made the poison for the Somali arrow, was here pointed out to us, and I have now with me a piece of it. Here, as in other places, extensive burial-grounds were observed, but, owing to the long drought, the people had retired to the mountains further inland, and, had we not taken the precaution of driving a few sheep with us from the sea, we should have been on very short-commons indeed.

Sunday morning afforded us a rest, but in the afternoon we pushed on for an hour, passing on our road many places where the track of the rhinoceros was recent. The cactus appears to be the favorite food of this animal, for we found many trees torn down and half eaten also. A beautiful red flower, too delicate to preserve, was here first observed. Specimens of red ochre, and fossil shells filled with the same, were to be picked up at every step; and the gum arabic had now replaced the luban or frankincense tree. Before sunset we halted on a plain immediately below the summit of the mountains, and were honored with the presence of the sister of Mahomed Ali Gerad, who, in company with a relation, was travelling to her home in the Wadi Nogál. The night was bitterly cold, the thermometer shewing a temperature of 48°, and the dew falling like soft rain. An occasional howl from the jungle warned us that leopards were to be found in the neighbourhood, and kept our Somali conductors on the qui vive; and we were not sorry to re-commence our journey at sunrise.

Sending the tent round by a more practicable road, we scaled the almost perpendicular cliff, rising some 750 feet above us, and by eight o'clock found ourselves on the summit of Eyransid, 6500 feet above the sea, and the first Europeans that had ever placed foot on the soil.

To describe the grandeur of the prospect before us is impossible. Range after range lay stretched like a map at our feet, and the view was bounded only by the ocean. The towns of Ras Kori and Sohm were to be seen dotted on the glaring sandy shore; and the *Euphrates* lay like a speck on the water. At noon the thermometer stood at 64°, and the sand driving past and below us, warned us to prepare for a cold night. As the afternoon advanced, the clouds packed heavy and thick below us, and the rocket and blue-light fired to notify our safety to our friends on board were consequently not seen at the ship.

To our surprise the temperature during the night was not so low as on the plain 800 feet below us—the thermometer standing at 52°: warm clothing was however indispensable, and our Somali guards peevishly remarked, that though we were always wishing for cold weather we did not appear inclined to benefit by it, judging from the blankets &c. that we were glad to creep under. As they had but a single cotton cloth themselves, some little excuse might be made for them; and a venerable old ram, purchased the next morning from a passing Dulbahanta Somali, restored them to their good honour. We spent the following day in wandering over the level plateau forming the summit of the range. The wild fig, twenty-five to thirty feet in height, was thinly scattered along the ridge.

The dragon's-blood tree was observed twenty-six inches in diameter, and eighteen feet in height. The ebony was plentiful, but of small size. A tree similar to, and possibly the lignum vitæ, attracted our notice; and cedar trees, some of them twenty-four inches in diameter and twenty-five feet high, were common. In cutting the cedar we observed that the wood which appeared to be growing had no scent, and was nearly white, whilst the more aged branches, that apparently bore no leaf, were of a very deep colour, and had a very strong perfume. The wood is neither prized or used by the Somalis.

Various and very beautiful wild flowers were scattered over the plain. The aloe of Socotra was abundant, and of good quality, but not used or known by the people. Many species of euphorbium and milk-bushes were seen, but no frankincense or gum arabic.

The summit of the range is composed of tabular masses of limestone, covered with small nodules, and very cellular, thereby rendering walking most uncomfortable, from the sharpness of the rock. At one point that we visited, a most magnificent natural wonder presented itself to us. A column of rock, of perhaps fifty feet square, had, by some convulsion of nature, been separated from the mountain side, and stood alone, a mighty pillar of 1500 feet in height, without hardly a break or irregularity in its sides, so straight had been the fracture. Trees, and the grass of years, remained on its summit untouched, the intervening fifty feet forming an impassable gulf; and at its foot, deep caverns went in far beneath the parent mountain, through whose windings a stone thrown down from above could be heard to reverberate long after it had passed from sight.

A second night of cloud and fog prevented again our communication with the brig by rocket or blue-light, but the " siraj," or light of the English, will long be held in remembrance by the Ahl Oor Sungeli, who could not sufficiently admire the one or the other. " You are the kings of this world in wisdom," said the solemn Mahammood Abdi, " and what are we in comparison? Thank heaven our world is to come !"

After a two days' stay in this delightful climate, we commenced the descent by the former route, intending to spend a day at the water 1000 feet below, and examine the frankincense trees in the neigbourhood.

Scrambling down the rock we passed many beautiful aloe trees of twenty feet in height, having several branches, and bearing a beautiful scarlet bell-flower, of the size and shape of the fox-glove. The aloe plant—the Socotra species—observed on the summit, bore a yellow flower, and of a different shape altogether. The camels that had been sent round as before, joined us with the melancholy tale of two of our sheep having been wounded by a leopard on their way down, and their having been obliged to cut their throats in consequence. Time unfortunately was too valuable to be lost, and we were compelled, though very unwillingly, to leave the culprit unpunished.

We halted at the water, under the shade of some gigantic fig-trees, laced together by an enormous creeper of some hundred feet in length, and probably caoutchouc trees. Rock partridges were here found, but no animals save Salt's white antelope, and hungry hyenas, who during the night made a meal off one of our water-skins. The frankincense found on the rocks over this spring was of the large leaf kind, known by the name of meyeti, and not much prized; but independently of gum arabic and frankincense, there were many other gum trees for which we could find no name. Of these, one, a specimen of which I brought to Aden, is, I feel sure, gum elemi; and another variety was shewn to us, the gum from which was used by the Somalis to cleanse the hair. To a botanist, these mountains would afford an inexhaustible field for research, and it is much to be hoped that the flora of the Somali coast may ere long be described in the manner that its beautiful varieties deserve.

On our return to Ras Kori, the chief town of the Ahl Oor Sungeli, we found that our unaccountable proceedings in the mountain range had excited much alarm. Amongst other wonderful stories, our having found the gold tree was confidently asserted; and it was significantly remarked that the English, by carrying away stones and trees from Aden when they surveyed the harbour, were enabled to capture the place afterwards with ease. Fearful, however, apparently of giving offence, the chief refrained from questioning us, and allowed us to repair on board without the slightest demur at the prices or presents that we thought sufficient recompense for his trouble.

The country of the Oor Sungeli may be described as a lofty plateau of limestone mountains, precipitous to the north, and gradually sloping to the south,—forming in fact a gunner's quoin. Between the mountains and the sea, undulating ranges occur, intersected by ravines, and thickly wooded; whilst the belt of level ground near the sea is thinly sprinkled with bushes, and exhibiting a plain of white sand. The Oor Sungeli country extends from Bunder Zeyadeh to Bunder Jedid.

The tribe is powerful and warlike. Brothers of the Mijirtheyn by the same mother, they generally coalesce should war break out, but petty feuds and plunder are of frequent occurrence.

The Oor Sungeli* are divided into several clans, of whom the following are the most important :—1st, Gerad Abdullah, the royal branch, from which the title of Gerad or chief descends by hereditary right. They reside on the sloping southern side of the great mountain range of Eyransid, or the " cloud-bearer." 2nd, the Noh Amor, who are found at Bunder Jedid. 3rd, Ogeiss Lubba, to whom belong two out of the three villages of Ras Kori. 4th, Aden Seyd, at the village of Galm, and the mountains above. 5th, Mayedth, resident at Doorderi. And lastly, the numerous clan of " Dubeiss," who occupy the towns of Elayeh, and extend to bunder Zeyadeh, where they join Mijirtheyn.

The Sultan Gerad Abdullah had three wives, who bore the three families of " Bha Mijirtheyn," " Bha Edoor," and " Bha Ogeiss Lubba." The present chief is of the Bha Mijirtheyn, or eldest, branch, and has now ruled for about three years. His power appears to be very great in some respects, and the sight of his baton, an ivory staff, is sufficient to collect the tribe in the event of war. But the chief to whose standard thousands would at once readily flock, dares not so much as fine, still less beat, any man of his tribe, unless supported by his elders.

The Oor Sungeli have numbers of horses, and of a good breed. With the exception of the tribe of Dubeiss, the arms used by them are the two spears and shield. The Dubeiss are nearly 5000 strong, and fight with the bow and poisoned arrow alone. It is worthy of remark, that in this tribe theft is looked upon with abhorrence, and though, in the event of a wreck, the natives would doubtless consider it fair to plunder, still, during my stay amongst them, though many a tempting opportunity of pilfering occurred, not an article was lost. To call a man a thief is a deadly insult, to be washed out by blood alone. Pity is it that the Somali tribes of the Edoor have not the same prejudice in favor of honesty.

* Bringer of good news.

It is a mistake supposing that the high ranges produce the best frank-incense. As before stated, we found no luban trees on the summit of Eyransid, though at an elevation of two to 3000 feet they were abundant. The traveller in crossing the Somali country generally is struck with the appearance of boundary lines dividing the hills into portions. These landmarks have existed probably for centuries, and serve to denote the limits of each family's gum-trees. In the Oor Sungeli tribes, we were assured that the gum-trees were never planted, but increased in course of nature. In the Mijirtheyn country we observed several young trees that had been transplanted, and we were then told that in some districts the trees were regularly cultivated like the coffee, and, naturally, the produce was increased seven-fold.

Frankincense, myrrh, sumuk or gum arabic, shenneh (orchel,) and ghee, form the exports of this tribe, and a peculiar kind of gum called " telleh felleh." I could not find the tree producing this gum, and I can hardly fancy, from the specimens in my possession, that it is the Persian fulay falah, the fruit of the aloe tree, as Richardson gives it in his dictionary. It is imported into Aden in large quantities from the coast, but the merchants cannot tell me the use made of it.

The graves found in the Somali country generally, and especially amongst the tribes of the Ahl Oor Sungeli, are remarkable for their neatness, being built of while slabs of limestone, almost marble, and sur-rounded by a circle of stones, the space within being neatly gravelled; but at Bunder Khor, in the Mijirtheyn territory, and in the neighbourhood of Berbera, very ancient graves are found consisting of a heap of stones, frequently seven to eight feet in height, and fifteen to eighteen feet in diameter at the base, hollowed in the centre, and with no head-stone ; similar in all respects to those described by Mr. Richardson in his "Travels in the Great Desert of the Sahara." They are, I fancy, relics of the Galla tribes, who once resided on the coast, but we could obtain no information regarding them.

To a traveller wishing to ascend the mountain ranges of the Jebel Ahl Oor Sungeli, I should recommend the small port of Doorderi, to the eastward of Ras Kori, as the best starting point. The mountain spurs there approach nearer the sea, and there is not the same scarcity of water: moreover, that part of the mountain district called Minneh, on which the people throughout the year keep immense herds of horned cattle, lies in his way. I do not anticipate any difficulty being thrown in the way by the chiefs, nor would the journey be very expensive; whilst the bracing climate, pure air, and magnificent scenery, must prove most advantageous to an invalid.

The Mijirtheyn Tribe has already been described by me in a Memoir forwarded to Government in 1843, and on looking over my notes, I do not find it requisite to make any alteration, excepting in one or two minor points. The luban meyeti is described as being the most valuable species of frankincense, which I have since ascertained not to be the case; and again, where the Mijirtheyn tribe are spoken of as inferior to the Western Somalis. A few years more experience has proved to me that the Mijirtheyn and Ahl Oor Sungeli tribes are immeasurably superior to those of the Edoor, and, though given to plunder a wreck, (a fault sometimes found in England), they will not rob the stranger of his own private property, and life is safe amongst them. With this very brief tribute to the manly character of the Mijirtheyn, I will now pass on to Ras Hafoon, the southern extreme of my wanderings on the Somali coast.

Ras Hafoon, or "the surrounded," is in the Mijirtheyn territory, and tenanted by Aial Fatha branch of the family of Othman. It consists of a nearly square headland of 600 to 700 feet in height, formed of sandstone and limestone. The outer edge of the peninsula is perfectly flat and tabular, and the interior consists of undulating hills, deeply intersected by ravines and the courses of mountain torrents. It is connected with the mainland by a long narrow neck of white sand, shells, and mud, with a few stunted bushes thinly scattered along it; and from its being thus almost an island, I imagine it takes its name Hafoon.

The southern bay is of course the best adapted for ships during the strength of the N. E. Monsoon, but a change of two or three points in the direction of the wind to the eastward causes a swell to roll in, and a surf to break on the beach. On our arrival there we found a few miserable Somali huts, and a population of perhaps fifty people, who offered ivory, ostrich-feathers, ambergris, and fish-teeth, for sale. The bay is much frequented by the shark-fishers from the Arabian coast, many of whom reside here throughout the year, merely moving their fishing-craft to the other side of the isthmus as the monsoon changes.

A walk of seven or eight miles brought us to the N. W. front of the cape, whence we embarked in a very crazy boat for the mainland. The bay, when we crossed, was too shallow for anything but very small vessels, and I feel confident that a ship would not be able to ride in safety through the S. W. Monsoon, owing to the heavy swell that must roll round the point, and the violent gusts of wind blowing across the head-land. This northern bay, or Khor Hoordea, I should imagine to be the most unhealthy spot on the Somali coast. Its shores and the bottom of the bay are covered with decomposed vegetable matter, which, on being disturbed, gives forth a noxious gas that is perfectly sickening, and in which the unfortunate traveller who longs for a bathe sinks leg deep; and yet we found many fishermen living on the sea shore, who, from long habit, had become accustomed to these exhalations, and wished for no better place.

We pursued our way for about nine miles to the Lagoon of Haudah, passing over a flat country, composed almost entirely of coral and lime-stone, and evidently at one time covered by the sea. At Haudah, to our great disappointment, we found the Lagoon salt water, except at its head, where it was barely drinkable. A well of good water was however found a few yards higher up, which shortly was crowded by the flocks and herds from the wooded plains inland of us. Our very uncommon appearance, the tent, and our baggage, occasioned unbounded astonish-ment to the natives, who poured in on every side, but no incivility was offered, and no article of our baggage was missing when we prepared to start on the following day. Milk was brought to us in abundance, which was paid for in blue cotton cloth; and sheep were equally attainable. Hafoon, however, like the whole Somali coast during the early part of 1848, was suffering from long-continued drought, which had occasioned much misery amongst them.

During the time that the French surveying vessels were anchored in the southern bay, in 1846, their crews cleared out one of the few wells found there, and thus procured a supply of good water. The other wells were brackish and bitter, and became deteriorated by constant use. In the northern bay, or Khor Hoordea, we found no water at all, but at the bottom of the bay, at a place called Khor Hashera, we were told that a stream of water ran into the sea. It is possible that the river mentioned by old writers as existing in the neighbourhood of Hafoon may be this stream, and Khor Hashera the ancient Opone.

During the S. W. Monsoon, a kind of fair, similar to that at Berbera, though much smaller, is annually observed at Khor Hoordea. The merchants from Maculla, Shahr, and from the Mijirtheyn Bunders to the northward and westward, attend this meeting about the end of May, when their bugalas are hauled up on the beach, and a brisk trade is carried on throughout the S. W. Monsoon, in gums, ostrich-feathers, hides, ivory, and ghee. Large quantities of ambergris are also brought for sale, and the price demanded is very great. Elephant hunting is followed by those who have guns, and last year upwards of thirty-five were killed by a party of gun-men brought by a speculating Somali from Brava, on the coast. A good trade might be carried on between Mauritius and Hafoon in donkeys. These could be procured at Hafoon in great numbers for five to six dollars each, and I should imagine consequently that the speculation would answer well, especially as the voyage would be so short in the N. E. Monsoon.

ADEN,
12th May, 1848.
⎱ (Signed.) C. J. CRUTTENDEN, *Lieutenant, I. N.,*
Assistant Political Agent, Aden.

(True Copy.) A. MALET, *Chief Secretary.*

www.ingramcontent.com/pod-product-compliance
Lightning Source LLC
Chambersburg PA
CBHW081307040426
42452CB00014B/2683

* 9 7 8 1 5 3 5 8 0 7 1 9 7 *